Eric

CW00551554

a Biography

Andrew Cooper

Published by A. Cooper Publications - 2011

A catalogue for this book is available from the British Library

ISBN 978-0-9568647-0-3

Printed & bound in the UK by Ashbourne Colour Print, Ilkeston, Derbyshire
Design, typography & layout by Tracy England
(tracy@haylandfreelance.com)

Typeset in CheltenhamBT

Front cover photo: **Eric making his daily inspection of the construction of the new North Stand**
Provided courtesy of Andrew Taylor

Back cover photo: **Team Photo Pre season 1959/60. Back in the top flight! A proud Eric deservedly shares the spotlight with his successor Harry Catterick. Every player signed by Eric!**
Provided courtesy of Derek Wilkinson

THIS BOOK IS DEDICATED TO MY FAMILY OF WEDNESDAYITES

MY LATE GRANDFATHER ALBERT, FATHER NORMAN & BROTHER JIM

Thanks to my grandfather & father, watching Wednesday has taught me how to cope with the ups and downs in life!

ABOUT THE AUTHOR

Andrew Cooper was born in Grenoside in 1949. At an early age he was taken by his father, a lifelong Wednesdayite, to watch reserve team matches at Hillsborough. In the mid 1950s he started attending first team games and, despite moving away from Sheffield in 1959, he has followed the Owls both at home and away up to the present day. As a teenager he played regularly for Pudsey Juniors as well as playing in Wednesday's reserve team forward line alongside Jack Whitham. After working for the Total Oil Company at its distribution depots in Leeds and Nottingham he retired in 2007 and now lives in Kimberley.

FOREWORD

Eric Taylor was part of my boyhood. In the early 1940s, I would see him most days as he cycled off from home in the morning - doubling up his job at Hillsborough with essential war work in the steel industry. His house - in Sheffield patois, 'four doors away' from ours - became famous in the locality when, after he was promoted and became Sheffield Wednesday Secretary, he had it painted blue and white. When I went to camp with the local Scout Troop he, or Mrs Taylor, gave me a waterproof sleeping bag, stamped with the initials 'JR'. Despite my parents' denials, I persisted in believing that it had once belonged to Jackie Robinson - inside forward, English international and the first of my Wednesday heroes. Eric Taylor was still doing me favours twenty years later. In 1966, my father was too far back in the queue to get us Cup Final tickets. Then, at Eric Taylor's suggestion, the box-office 'found' two, still waiting to be sold.

Standing on Spion Kop every other Saturday, I never thought - and the men around me never suggested - that there was anything strange about a football manager with little or no football experience. Years later, Dennis Woodhead - a wing forward who became Wednesday's commercial manager - told me that the Taylor team talk before the match never amounted to more than 'Do your best. Good luck.' But we never thought of such things. His reign at Hillsborough was never questioned, even after the regular relegations in the 'yo-yo years.'

We admired Eric Taylor as a great football innovator. He was the first manager to install floodlights - in itself the beginning of a revolution.

And he began a trend that has escalated beyond what we then imagined possible by setting the record transfer fee. It was largely thanks to him Hillsborough hosted a semi-final almost every year. Eric Taylor was a quiet man - which is why his contribution to football is often overlooked. Wednesdayites - and football supporters who do not follow the Owls - should rejoice that his achievements have now been recognised.

ROY HATTERSLEY

ACKNOWLEDGEMENTS

Without the help of the following people this book would not have been possible. I have been received with courtesy and enthusiasm everywhere. All of the following were only too willing to tell me about the time they spent with Eric.

For an insight into two unique transfer deals I thank Ron Springett and Jackie Sewell. Ron kindly entertained me at Loftus Road when Wednesday were the opponents.

Quite honestly, I was awestruck when I visited Jackie Sewell. Here was that great player who had smashed the British transfer record and had played against the mighty Magyars.

Don Megson, Gerry Young, Alan Finney, David Ford, and Derek Wilkinson recalled their halcyon days. Derek also provided me with photos from his career history which he had expertly catalogued. Tommy Craig recounted how he was determined to prove to Eric and all Wednesdayites that the record transfer fee paid for a teenager was money well spent.

Isabel Brown, who served as Eric's secretary and portrayed a man who commanded great respect.

Ron Ward, who served as caretaker for many years under Eric at Hillsborough and described him as a perfect gentleman.

Ernest Barron and Johnny Quinn, who provided me with invaluable contacts.

Robert and Andrew Taylor, Eric's sons. Their memories of their father and their memorabilia have certainly equalled the thrill of coming face to face with my boyhood heroes.

My thanks also to Roy Hattersley for agreeing to contribute a Foreword to my book.

My thanks to Steve Thomas and Tracy England of Aluset Ltd, without whose help this book would not have been possible.

Last but not least, thanks to my wife Sue for the many hours spent typing and for tolerating my obsession!

INTRODUCTION

My love affair with Sheffield Wednesday began in the 1950s and I was lucky enough to witness part of the period referred to as the Golden Age of football. The subject of this book, Eric Woodhouse Taylor, was manager (correct title, Secretary/Manager) at the time and was in his fourth decade with the club. As a young lad growing up in Grenoside I was oblivious to the massive contribution he had made to this great club but the passing of the years has led me to believe that it was about time someone went into print to honour his memory and to inform younger fans of his great legacy.

I firmly believe his achievements have been undervalued and overlooked and my research has revealed fascinating facts about the man who dedicated his life to his beloved Wednesday.

Eric Woodhouse Taylor served Sheffield Wednesday Football Club in a career that spanned 6 decades! No one before or after him has contributed so much to the club. At a time when places in and around our magnificent stadium are being named after illustrious players of the past I find it unbelievable that he has not been included. Surely, Eric's greatest legacy is our stadium?

Eric's first association with Wednesday is expertly chronicled by John Brodie and Jason Dickinson in their book The Wednesday Boys (Pickard Communications, 2005). This publication is a must for all Wednesday fans.

This book is my tribute to Eric and if the reader gets half the pleasure that I have had in my research I will know it has been worthwhile.

I appreciate its circulation may not be as far reaching as other football biographies but the book is primarily aimed at the 'Football Man', for that is certainly my description of Eric. Having seen and heard what he achieved in the game and for the game, I find it astonishing that this service was not acknowledged at a national level. After all, service to football has been recognised at the highest level to far lesser mortals than Eric. But that's my opinion.

Without doubt, some of Wednesday's greatest players owe everything to Eric. His players were his 'family' and were treated as such. The same applies to the backroom staff. In all my conversations with former players and staff I have not heard one complaint about Eric. He was never chairman but the most telling comment I remembered was from his secretary.

Every time she mentioned Eric she referred to him as 'The Boss' and this title stuck well after he relinquished managerial duties.

Eric passed away in 1974. He never fully recovered after sustaining serious injuries in a horrendous road accident. It is no coincidence to my mind that when his guiding influence disappeared, the club entered a disastrous downward spiral that culminated in just avoiding the drop to the lowest league on the final day of the season of 1975/76. Wednesday had never been lower than the second tier in its history when it was relegated to the then 3rd Division in the season of 1974/75.

His administrative skills have never been doubted but I will endeavour to recall how he dealt with the major disappointments of the Dooley tragedy and the bribes scandal of the 60s. His leadership at these times was critical. I will also, more interestingly, detail how his knowledge of the game was far more profound than players and fans alike thought it to be.

Kimberley, Notts.

January 2011

CHAPTER ONE

FROM OFFICE BOY TO MANAGER

Eric was born in Fulwood and spent his formative years in the suburb of Birley Carr only a stone's throw from Hillsborough. The Chairman at the time of Eric's appointment as office boy was none other than Sir Charles Clegg, a giant in the game locally and nationally. Sir Charles's reputation as an administrator was second to none. He had played the game at the highest level, gaining international caps, and after retiring from playing he turned to refereeing where he officiated at cup finals. Little would Sir Charles imagine at the time, that Eric would himself become one of the game's great administrators. Eric would also witness another club chairman, Dr. Andrew Stephen, (later to become Sir Andrew Stephen) follow in the footsteps of Sir Charles in being appointed FA Chairman, thus continuing the club's longstanding tradition of providing the men who were to have such a massive influence on the national game. Indeed, it can be said that Dr Stephen received great support from Eric, which must have impressed the selection committee. Eric even cancelled an overseas tour in order to accompany Dr Stephen to an FA committee meeting and to offer as much support as possible.

The 1920s couldn't have been much fun for a teenager. The memory of the Great War would still have been in everyone's mind, with football serving as a safety valve and an escape from the austerity of those times.

Unfortunately, Eric would witness exactly the same scenario after the second World War.

After his appointment as office boy in 1929, Eric must have been swept along with the exciting times that prevailed at Hillsborough. The 1929/30 season saw the club retain the Division 1 title. He would then witness the 1935 FA Cup Final victory. True halcyon days which have not been equalled in 75 years.

The second World War saw the suspension of the established League and Cup competitions and clubs could only make the numbers up by having guest players.

Naturally, many players were called up and could only appear when on leave. The war meant that football, in effect, was being run on a part time basis.

Jimmy McMullan, who had so nearly guided the club back to Division 1 in the last full season before the war (pipped by Sheffield United by one point!) was unlucky to be told that his contract would not be renewed in 1942.

These were worrying times for everyone and the Chairman, William Turner, was convinced that the workload had to be spread amongst the remaining staff at the club. Eric was now employed as assistant secretary but he was asked to take on extra responsibility in the form of part time manager of team affairs. One can only assume that he had shown interest in team matters as he accepted the challenge. Eric's decision led to his being in charge of team affairs for 16 years! Surely his elevation was only meant as a temporary measure?

Things would revert to normal after the war? He obviously relished the chance to prove that the Chairman and his Board of Directors had made the right decision. In 1943 he led the club to the Northern League Cup Final. Wednesday were narrowly beaten over two legs, but Eric had made his mark. The end of the war finally came and in 1945 Chairman William Fearnehough rewarded him with a new contract and title of Secretary/Manager.

A young Eric (seated 2nd left bottom) attending Golden Jubilee celebration of the Football League

Photo provided courtesy of Andrew Taylor

4

DIVISION 2 1938-39

Blackburn Rovers	42	25	5	12	94	60	55
Sheffield United	42	20	14	8	69	41	54
Sheffield Wednesday	42	21	11	10	88	59	53
Coventry City	42	21	8	13	62	45	50
Manchester City	42	21	7	14	96	72	49
Chesterfield	42	20	9	13	69	52	49
Luton Town	42	22	5	15	82	66	49
Tottenham Hotspur	42	19	9	14	67	62	47
Newcastle United	42	18	10	14	61	48	46
West Bromwich Albion	42	18	9	15	89	72	45
West Ham United	42	17	10	15	70	52	44
Fulham	42	17	10	15	61	55	44
Millwall	42	14	14	14	64	53	42
Burnley	42	15	9	18	50	56	39
Plymouth Argyle	42	15	8	19	49	55	38
Bury	42	12	13	17	65	74	37
Bradford Park Avenue	42	12	11	19	61	82	35
Southampton	42	13	9	20	56	82	35
Swansea Town	42	11	12	19	50	83	34
Nottingham Forest	42	10	11	21	49	82	31
Norwich City	42	13	5	24	50	91	31
Tranmere Rovers	42	6	5	31	39	99	17

Division 2 league table, 1938/39. Not happy reading for Wednesday fans
Provided courtesy of John Brodie

5

CHAPTER TWO

BRITISH TRANSFER RECORDS SMASHED

All the players I spoke to when researching this book said that they didn't think Eric had any influence on team affairs such as tactics and selection. They were at pains to point out that he was never seen at the training ground, let alone in a track suit. The coaching staff were responsible for the daily training sessions and the team for the Saturday game would be pinned up in the dressing room on the Friday.

The 1950s began with Wednesday returning to the top division. Local youngsters Quixall and Finney had signed professional forms and were soon to establish themselves in the team. No doubt the club had a well established scouting system, but on talking to Eric's sons I was to discover that those players, and probably thousands of supporters, were completely oblivious to the fact that Eric travelled far and wide watching players. Andrew and Robert Taylor remember that Sunday was the only day that they spent with their father and that included being taken to Hillsborough where they enjoyed the freedom of running on the pitch and exploring the ground while their father completed some administrative work. Then it was home for Sunday dinner. They said their father was out Monday to Friday, either watching players or negotiating transfers, and by the time he returned home the two lads were tucked up in bed.

After hearing this, there was no doubt in my mind that Eric's reputation as being solely an administrator was incorrect and I was now confident that my opinion regarding his influence on football matters was being substantiated. Quixall, Finney and Froggatt, along with Swan, Megson, Wilkinson, Young, Dooley, Jim and Tom McAnearney, Kay and Fantham, were all signed by Eric. They all had great careers. Furthermore, Eric was to prove that Wednesday was a force in the

Albert Quixall
Photo provided, courtesy of P. Gordon

land by being involved in three record transfer deals in the 1940s and 1950s. Eddie Quigley was sold in 1949 for a record fee (£26,500). Nearly ten years later Albert Quixall went to Manchester United for £45,000.

It is also worth mentioning that Eric paid £20,000 (a record for a winger) to Bury in 1948 to capture the services of Eddie Kilshaw.

Eddie was quick to make an impression but an injury sustained after only 19 appearances ended his career. In between these years there was the record signing of Jackie Sewell from Notts County for £35,000.

As I mentioned earlier, I had the great privilege of meeting Jackie, who gave me a fascinating insight into the story of the transfer.

What follows, in my opinion, encapsulates the attitudes that prevailed at the time. I contacted Jackie via his old club, Notts County, and he invited me to this home, a modest bungalow, unlike the trappings of today's top professionals. On the sideboard were displayed the reminders of his halcyon days, including a photograph of him in his England shirt and wearing his international cap. Here was someone who had played against the mighty Magyars, thrilled thousands of Wednesdayites, and helped win the FA Cup for Aston Villa.

The story of his transfer unfolded and one man only persuaded Jackie to end his partnership with his great friend Tommy Lawton, and that man was Eric Taylor.

Jackie had just returned to Meadow Lane after a training session when he was told that a Mr Taylor wished to speak to him. His manager at Notts County, Eric Houghton, informed Jackie that Mr Taylor was from Sheffield Wednesday and that he wanted to sign him. Jackie's response was not very encouraging for Eric. He was extremely happy playing alongside Tommy Lawton and had no wish to move to Sheffield. What was to follow demonstrated that the players in those days had no say in transfer negotiations and the final decision was made by directors of the club. His manager was keen to keep Jackie but he was despatched to watch the second team while Jackie, Eric and the directors in favour of the sale retired to a hotel in Nottingham.

It was transfer deadline day so the deal had to be completed before 8 p.m. to allow him to play for his new club for the remainder of the season. Jackie remained obdurate and tried unsuccessfully to contact his friend, Tommy Lawton, for advice. Eventually, he signed on the dotted line just before the deadline. His manager, who was desperate to keep him, dashed into the hotel after being kept out of the negotiations deliberately, only to learn that Jackie had signed for Wednesday.

When I asked why he had changed his mind Jackie said it was because Eric Taylor was so persuasive, but also that Eric was a gentleman and had treated him impeccably. I also learned that one of Notts County's directors who was opposed to the sale drove up to Sheffield the next day to return the cheque and to tell Eric that the transfer was null and void. Needless to say, he was unsuccessful in his attempt to keep Jackie. Eric had got his man! Jackie was never told what the fee was!

So Jackie's account of his transfer clearly emphasises Eric's powers of persuasion. Post war Sheffield was a hard sell with the steel works and heavy industry belching out their pollution. The most direct route to Hillsborough from the two railway stations took any strangers to the city past an industrial landscape. Eric, however, ensured that the journey to Hillsborough followed a route taking in the more attractive suburbs approaching Hillsborough via Rivelin Valley or Walkley.

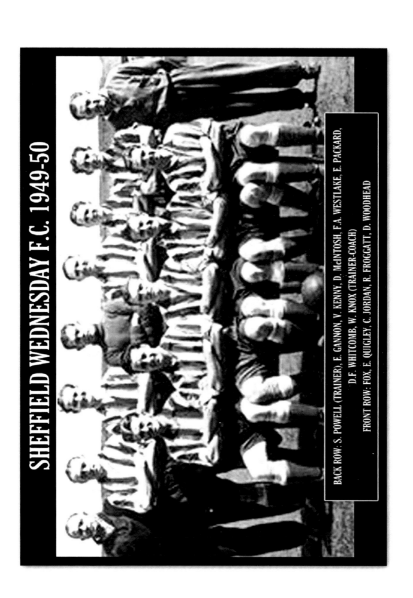

SHEFFIELD WEDNESDAY F.C. 1949-50

BACK ROW: S. POWELL (TRAINER), E. GANNON, V. KENNY, D. McINTOSH, F.A. WESTLAKE, E. PACKARD,
D.F. WHITCOMB, W. KNOX (TRAINER-COACH)

FRONT ROW: FOX, E. QUIGLEY, C. JORDAN, R. FROGGATT, D. WOODHEAD

Division 2 promotion winning team 1949/50

Photo provided courtesy of Derek Wilkinson

11

1956

SHEFFIELD WEDNESDAY

BACK ROW: FROGGATT, HILL, PINNER, O'DONNEL, FINNEY
FRONT ROW: QUIXALL, MARTIN, McANEARNEY, WILKINSON, SHINER, CURTIS

Division 2 promotion winning team 1955/56 minus goalkeeper Dave McIntosh. Mike Pinner
played as an amateur as replacement for injured professionals. Mike's parent club was Pegasus
Photo provided courtesy of Derek Wilkinson

12

CHAPTER THREE

THE FATHER FIGURE

There is no doubt that Eric regarded all who worked for him at Hillsborough as his 'family'. That included the players, staff and everyone else connected with the club. I have spoken to his secretary, Isabel Brown, and caretaker Ron Ward who both gave many years service under Eric and had the utmost respect for him. Eric would always have a kind word and appreciated anyone who gave 100%. His secretary told me of the many high profile figures in the game who were in regular contact with Eric, such as Sir Stanley Rous, Joe Richards, Matt Busby, Bill Nicholson, Alan Hardaker and members of the press. His caretaker can only remember the one time when Eric was visibly upset and that was the day that the bribes scandal, involving David Layne, Peter Swan and Tony Kay, came to light.

Don Megson recounted how Eric had both nurtured his career and given him invaluable advice when his playing days were coming to an end. Don had struggled to gain a place in the first team under Eric after signing in 1954. However, Eric had managed to persuade his friend, Matt Busby, to allow Don to train with Manchester United when he couldn't make the journey from his home in Lancashire to Hillsborough. Eric also ensured that Don remained in this country when he undertook his national service, so that he was available for games if needed. Don broke into the first team under Harry Catterick and never looked back.

When his playing career came to an end, Eric's contacts in the game helped him take up the position of player coach and ultimately manager at Bristol Rovers. Don had received other more lucrative offers but decided to take Eric's advice, for which he has been eternally grateful.

John Quinn also remembered how Eric would organise travel arrangements for him from abroad, where he was doing his national service. Everything was organised down to the last detail to ensure that John was available.

Alan Finney told me about the overseas tours that were organised by Eric. Every player was allocated a certain amount of spending money.

There were quite a few occasions when this ran out but Eric was quite easily persuaded to hand out more. Alan recalled how he missed a team meeting along with a colleague on one of the tours. It was the only time he ever received a reprimand from Eric but he recognised that it was fully deserved.

Another player who owes Eric so much is Ron Springett. His transfer from QPR to Wednesday soon saw him establish himself as a regular custodian in the international team, gaining more England caps than any other Wednesday player before or since. His transfer was also unique, as I will endeavour to record. Ron invited me to Loftus Road when the Owls played there. It was a day I shall never forget.

He talked about his transfer and then I sat beside him to watch the game. Research for this book has been quite daunting at times. Meeting up with my childhood heroes has been amazing, especially when Ron produced the letter I had written to him over 40 years ago, thanking him for his service to the Owls!

Ron had heard that Sunderland were keen to sign him and had told him that he could remain down south and continue training with QPR. Eric was desperate for Ron to sign as Wednesday were in danger of being relegated. Ron had just bought his first house and had decided to get married so didn't want to be rushed. However, Eric's persistence paid off eventually and Ron accepted the same terms that Sunderland had offered which meant he could stay down south. Unfortunately, Ron was to experience relegation soon after joining. You will note from the reprinted letter that Eric wrote to him much later, how he believed that Ron's delay in signing was a contributory factor in Wednesday's relegation that season. Ron's first full season saw the club bounce straight back and remain in the top flight for a further 10 years. Eric had prophesied that Ron would be a full international within two to three years. The records show that this came true after only 18 months! Yet another example of Eric's being able to spot talent in a player. Ron went on to become the most capped England international in the club's history. His 33 caps remains a record today. He played in the 1962 World Cup in Chile and was a squad member in 1966 as an understudy to the lad from Sheffield, Gordon Banks.

Ron, like many of his playing colleagues, described Eric as a gentleman and if he did have a weakness, he was too easy going with the players. He was also at pains to point out to me that the club only once tried to renege on the terms of his contract. Vic Buckingham was to demand that Ron move to Sheffield in 1964 but Eric had the last word and insisted that the terms agreed could not be broken. Not long after this confrontation Vic Buckingham's reign as manager ended.

Ron was keen to point out that the 9 years spent at Hillsborough were the happiest in his career. It was Ron who used the phrase 'Father Figure' when referring to Eric.

SHEFFIELD WEDNESDAY 1958 HILLSBOROUGH

BACK ROW: MARTIN, FANTHAM, McANEARNY, SPRINGETT, WILKINSON, GIBSON, SWAN
FRONT ROW: FINNEY, FROGGATT, SHINER, CURTIS

Division 2 promotion winning team 1958/59

Photo provided courtesy of Derek Wilkinson

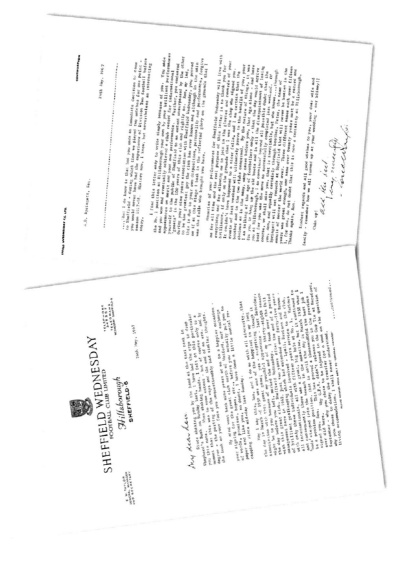

Letter from Eric Taylor to Ron Springett 1967

Provided courtesy of Ron Springett

Eric with some of the "family" at the seaside. (Early 1960s)
L to R: Johnny Fantham, Jack Mansell (coach), Vic Mobley, Ron Springett,
Gerry Young, Peter Eustace.

Photo provided courtesy Andrew Taylor

CHAPTER FOUR

THE CATTERICK REIGN

Eric was in full agreement with his board of directors when it was decided that he should step down as team manager in 1958. There were massive challenges ahead and he threw himself into the work of modernising Hillsborough. Before standing down he was to witness a unique and sombre occasion. In February of that year the football world was stunned, when the plane returning home with the Manchester United entourage from a European tie, crashed attempting a take off at Munich airport. 21 people perished including 7 players. Manchester United's first opponents following the disaster were Sheffield Wednesday. It was the 5th round of the FA Cup. The whole nation was gripped in a groundswell of sympathy. Manchester United were allowed to make emergency signings in order to stage the game. As a mark of respect the Manchester United team in the programme appeared as 11 blank spaces. Matt Busby lay in bed fighting for his life. Wednesday faced a mission impossible. The game ended in a 3-0 defeat for Wednesday but thanks to Eric's leadership and dignified approach in such a charged atmosphere the club received widespread praise from the football fraternity. So after 16 years in charge of team affairs he was replaced by Harry Catterick as team manager. Catterick had played for Everton and had cut his managerial teeth at Crewe and Rochdale.

It is worth noting that before Catterick's appointment the Wednesday board, acting on Eric's advice, had approached Bill Nicholson but after a lengthy deliberation, Yorkshireman Bill decided to stay at Tottenham. How ironic that the team he built there went on to become Wednesday's nemesis in that memorable season 1960/61 when Tottenham won the coveted League and Cup double for the first time in the century and Wednesday finished runners-up. However, thousands of Owls fans did have the consolation of seeing their team become the first team to beat Tottenham in a memorable match at Hillsborough that season.

It was during Catterick's reign as manager that, I believe, Eric received unjust criticism from a large section of supporters. Speak to many fans of my age today and the majority would probably say that Eric prevented Catterick from winning the League title because he wouldn't loosen the purse strings to provide the manager with a transfer kitty. A popular accusation at the time and since was, 'Eric put ground improvements before success on the field'. At that time Hillsborough was recognised as one of, if not the, most important stadiums outside Wembley.

For years it had hosted semi-finals and the odd international. Eric had gained a great reputation as a brilliant organiser and administrator as these important games passed without incident and brought in massive receipts for both the FA and the club. I learned that Eric used to listen to the semi-final draw and would rub his hands together as he knew that Hillsborough would be allocated a tie.

Catterick wasted no time in making his mark as he steered Wednesday back to Division 1 in his first season. The following season saw the club finish a respectable 5th in the highest division but Catterick realised that this could be bettered. He was proved correct when in the next season Wednesday finished runners up to the mighty double winning Spurs. After his arrival in 1958 Catterick made only 3 signings. Of those only one would make a substantial impact: Bobby Craig (£6,500 from Third Lanark). George Kirby never established himself and quickly moved on and John Quinn had to wait several years before gaining a regular 1st team slot. In other words, the team that stormed back to Division 1 and then narrowly missed out on the League title was the team that Eric Taylor had assembled. Eric had been criticised after the record transfer of local hero Albert Quixall to Manchester United but local product Johnny Fantham soon proved to be a capable replacement.

Don Megson told me that Catterick was always asking for more money and genuinely thought that Joe Baker, the Hibernian centre forward, was the missing piece of his plan to clinch the league title. Ultimately, after relations between himself and Eric deteriorated, Catterick departed and joined the millionaire set at Everton. We will never know if that one player (Joe Baker) would have brought the success that all Wednesdayites were hoping for but I would ask all of you to peruse the playing statistics of Keith Ellis, who led the attack after Wednesday regained Division 1 status in 1959. Keith had his most successful seasons back in the top flight.

The statistics reveal that he made 116 appearances in league and cup, scoring 59 goals including a hat trick at Old Trafford! Give me a centre forward today who can better a goal every other game!

The records show we won nothing but it's worth repeating what Don Megson said. In his opinion, the team that finished runners up to Spurs was the best team he ever played in. Apart from Bobby Craig every one of those players was either discovered and nurtured or signed by Eric Taylor.

Harry Catterick went on to taste the success he craved for at Hillsborough, leading Everton to a League title and a Cup Final victory over his old employers. He also persuaded Tony Kay to join him after paying a record fee for a half back. All this success was ammunition for the Eric Taylor critics and his actions during Catterick's time as team manager will always remain a contentious issue among the older generation of Wednesday supporters.

BACK ROW: TOMMY EGGELSTON (TRAINER) DEREK WILKINSON, DON MEGSON, PETER SWAN, RON SPRINGETT, TONY KAY.
PETER JOHNSON AND TOMMY McANEARNEY
FRONT ROW: ALAN FINNEY, KEITHELLIS, HARRY CATTERICK (MANAGER), BOBBY CRAIG AND JOHN FANTHAM

FOOTBALL LEAGUE DIVISION 1 RUNNERS UP 1960-1

Division 1 runners up 1960/61. (Bobby Craig only player in team signed by Harry Catterick)

Provided courtesy of Derek Wilkinson

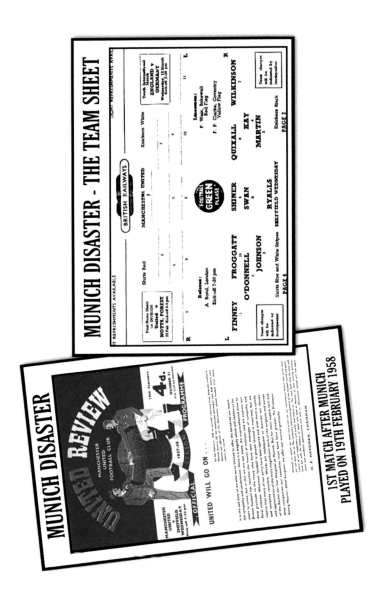

Manchester Utd. v Wednesday programme cover first game after Munich disaster

Team sheet from programme

Provided courtesy of Derek Wilkinson

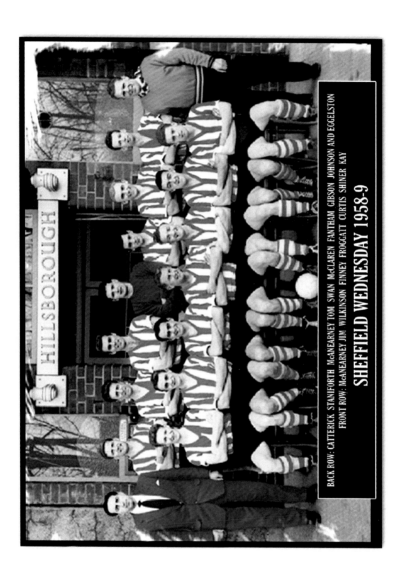

BACK ROW: CATTERICK STANIFORTH McANEARNEY TOM SWAN McCLAREN FANTHAM GIBSON JOHNSON AND EGGELSTON
FRONT ROW: McANEARNEY JIM WILKINSON FINNEY FROGGATT CURTIS SHINER KAY

SHEFFIELD WEDNESDAY 1958-9

Promotion winning team 1958/59

Provided courtesy of Derek Wilkinson

Programme cover of FA Cup 4th round replay, Manchester Utd. v Wednesday 1961.
(Wednesday triumphed 7-2!)
Newspaper cuttings recording Keith Ellis' proudest moment as a Wednesday player after scoring
a hat-trick
All provided courtesy of Derek Wilkinson

CHAPTER FIVE

HIS DARKEST HOURS

Derek Dooley was playing for Lincoln City as an amateur when he was signed by Eric in 1947. Derek was a Sheffield lad and had played for the local YMCA. More importantly, he was an ardent Wednesdayite in a city with divided loyalties.

Ironically, Derek made his debut for Wednesday against Preston N.E. in March 1950. The following season saw him make only the one appearance again but in the season 1951/52 he marked his first appearance in the league against Barnsley with 2 goals. Derek had 'arrived'. He went on to score 47 goals in 31 appearances (League and Cup), a record which still stands for a Wednesday player. These goals were scored in Division 2 and many of his critics prophesied a much leaner time for Derek in Division 1. How wrong they were to be proved! Up to his career ending injury at Preston he had made 30 appearances and scored 16 goals. His club statistics read: 61 appearances, 62 goals!

Every Wednesday fan knows that Derek had a leg amputated after gangrene infected his wound. Fans at the time were inconsolable. He had terrorised defences up and down the land. What would the future hold? No doubt at the instigation of Eric and the board of directors, the club ensured that Derek would be helped. After a lengthy period of rehabilitation at the local limb fitting centre in

Handsworth Derek began his struggle to adapt to life outside the game.

After working for a national newspaper his next job was at a local bakery which was owned by a director on the board at Hillsborough, Mr. Gunstone. In 1955 he was awarded a testimonial game. His tragic accident touched the nation and he featured on 'This Is Your Life' hosted by Eamon Andrews. It wasn't long before he returned to Hillsborough where he worked tirelessly as Development Fund Manager. In 1971 he accepted what turned out to be the poisoned chalice when he succeeded Danny Williams as team manager. At this time Eric was still recovering from his serious road accident in 1967 and his influence was waning. My research has indicated that Eric was not over enthusiastic about Derek's appointment. Eric had great affection for him and held him in high esteem, but perhaps he foresaw the harsh treatment that befell him when he was sacked on Christmas Eve by the then chairman Matt Sheppard. It led Derek to desert his beloved Owls and transfer his allegiance to the Blades across the city. To this day, Derek's widow still refuses to visit Hillsborough!

Derek's fate was repeated when a junior player, Dougie McMillan, also had a leg amputated after the team coach crashed on returning from Arsenal on Boxing Day 1960. Once again Eric and the board did all they could to support Dougie.

The early 1960s saw Wednesday establish themselves in Division 1 after they stormed to promotion in 1959. No one at the time could have prophesied the bombshell which was to rip the team apart a few years later. Vic Buckingham, who succeeded Harry Catterick, had made his name as a coach on the continent.

In six seasons, after promotion in 1959, Wednesday had never finished lower than 8th in the top division. The team was full of stars. Springett and Swan were established internationals. Fantham and Young would also gain international honours. Undoubtedly, Buckingham's best signing was David 'Bronco' Layne. Wednesday played some delightful football and Layne scored 32 goals in his first season. Gerry Young recalled how Buckingham was responsible for converting him into a half back. A position that he commanded for 7 years. Gerry had earlier in his career emulated Keith Ellis by scoring a hat-trick as a centre forward against Manchester United! For a short spell the forward line resembled an American western cast when Mark 'Pancho' Pearson played alongside 'Bronco' after the signing of this former 'Busby Babe' from Old Trafford.

On December 1st 1962 Wednesday played a routine away fixture at Ipswich which resulted in a 2-0 defeat. Little did anyone know or suspect at the time that this game was to lead to amazing revelations which would stun the footballing world and subsequently curtail brilliant careers in the game for 3 household names. There were many other players involved in the betting scam which came to be known as the 'football bribes scandal' but the 3 household names were those of Sheffield Wednesday players. Tony Kay had moved on to Everton to team up with his former manager Harry Catterick, but along with Peter Swan and 'Bronco' Layne he was found guilty of placing a bet for Wednesday to lose on that day at Ipswich. Ironically, Kay had been named 'Man of the Match' for the Owls by a popular Sunday newspaper but this didn't wash with the football establishment or the jury at their subsequent trial. As if a jail sentence was not enough, a life ban from the game was handed down by the FA in 1964.

At a stroke the team lost an established international centre half who would, probably, have represented his country in the World Cup in 1966 as well as a prolific goalscorer in David Layne. Tony Kay had just gained international honours at Everton and no doubt the Merseyside club were aggrieved after paying Wednesday a record fee for a half back!

Everyone connected with the club was stunned when the revelations appeared in a Sunday newspaper. None more so than Eric. In an earlier chapter I referred to comments made by the caretaker at the time. He had never seen Eric so low. Eric's sons also recalled in great detail the Sunday when the news broke. The phone never stopped ringing at home. They told me that they had never seen their father so agitated. On the Monday after the Sunday press had broken the news the Owls played Spurs at Hillsborough. Swan and Layne did not appear and Eric gave a speech over the public address system at half time stating that these were dark days for the club but it was 'Churchillian' in the way it galvanised everyone to pull together.

The team, roared on by a passionate crowd, responded magnificently by beating Spurs 2-0. Derek Wilkinson scored both goals as a stand in centre forward and Vic Mobley made his home debut as a replacement for Peter Swan.

Derek Wilkinson was one of those true professionals and told me that his time spent at Hillsborough was the happiest of his career.

Derek also had to suffer the heartbreak of a sudden end to his career. At 29, playing against Manchester United at Old Trafford, he tore his groin, which resulted in the removal of an abductor muscle. He never kicked a ball in anger again! He told me how his worry about his sudden fall in earnings was cushioned when Eric informed him that the club would offer financial support. Derek was subsequently granted a testimonial, a fitting reward for a player who had given his all for the club.

Vic Mobley went on to establish himself in the team and became a hero in the semi-final victory over Chelsea in 1966 by staying on the pitch as nuisance value after sustaining an injury which prevented him playing in the final and gaining full international honours. The injury meant a premature end to his career after moving to QPR, who subsequently attempted to sue Wednesday.

Don Megson recalled the time of the bribes scandal vividly. He stated how it was obvious to all close to Eric that he was deeply affected by events, but he insisted that Eric's handling of the situation led to an even greater respect for him. In a strange way Don thought that the turmoil that engulfed the club was a catalyst for Eric, in as much as he was determined that 'his' club's image would not be irrevocably tarnished by these unsavoury events.

Of course, relegation from the top flight in 1970 was another dark day for Eric but this pales into insignificance compared with the personal tragedies described and the adverse publicity that the club received after the bribes scandal was exposed. I was told that Eric visited Peter, David and Tony in jail and in 1972 both Peter and David were welcomed back to the club when their life bans were lifted. So, along with his concern for the future welfare of Derek Dooley, Derek Wilkinson and Dougie McMillan after the premature end to their careers, we see a man who was both forgiving and caring.

TOM FINNEY AND TOMMY DOCHERTY VISIT DEREK DOOLEY IN HOSPITAL
1953

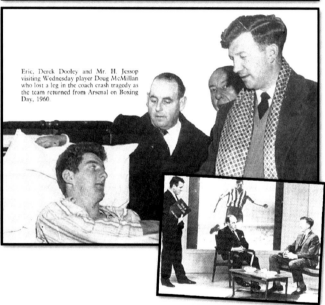

Eric, Derek Dooley and Mr. H. Jessop visiting Wednesday player Doug McMillan who lost a leg in the coach crash tragedy as the team returned from Arsenal on Boxing Day, 1960.

Derek Dooley receiving distinguished visitors in hospital in Preston

Photo provided, courtesy of Derek Wilkinson

A case of deja vu. Derek doing the visiting alongside Eric and a director after Dougie McMillan suffered the same fate 7 years later

Photo provided, courtesy of Sheffield Wednesday

Derek Dooley appearing on 'This Is Your Life' hosted by Eamon Andrews

Photo provided courtesy of Sheffield Wednesday

Newspaper cuttings reporting on first game after the 'bribes scandal' broke. Wednesday v Spurs. Derek Wilkinson replaced David Layne at centre forward and scored both goals in a 2-0 victory

Provided courtesy of Derek Wilkinson

CHAPTER SIX

THE MOTIVATOR

A happy and contented workforce, as we all know, is a pre-requisite for success in any line of business. My research has highlighted that during Eric's tenure at Hillsborough this was definitely true. Everyone I have spoken to, staff and players alike, has been at pains to emphasise how happy they were.

Eric's great passion for the club was obvious for all to see. Loyalty is not a word synonymous with the modern game, but it meant so much to Eric. He genuinely believed that Sheffield Wednesday was the best club in the land and his staff and players were treated in such a way that they also believed it was the best to work and play for.

Eric's secretary and the club's caretaker recalled the 1966 Cup Final and the centenary celebrations in 1967. No expense was spared. The post Cup Final banquet was held at the Russell Hotel in London. There were no fewer than 258 guests! These included members of the 1935 Cup winning team, leading dignitaries in the world of football and Sheffield public service and everyone employed at Hillsborough. There were two guests representing Reading Football Club, the team Wednesday had beaten in the 3rd round. Eric didn't leave anyone out!

The club was 100 years old on the 5th September 1967 and the team celebrated in great style the next day by beating Fulham 4-2.

By way of celebrating this great milestone, rumour has it that the club wished to admit supporters free of charge to the Fulham game but the Football League refused to sanction this. As a compromise fans were admitted at a reduced price.

I was told that an away fixture in London was something that was always greeted with enthusiasm. Without fail the team plus entourage would travel down on the Friday and would take in a show in the west end. All the players knew that their fierce rivals across the city travelled to London games and returned the same day!

Another highlight in the calendar was the end of season tour. You will recall how, in an earlier chapter, Alan Finney had happy memories of these. Alan showed me the little rule book issued to every player before a pre-season tour. Central America, Africa, Europe, the Far East, Russia were all visited. On many occasions, games were played in packed stadia.

David Ford recalled the time when the team's hotel was besieged with hundreds of fans in Mexico. David was amazed, thinking that the fans were waiting for the Wednesday team to emerge but his misplaced superiority complex evaporated quickly when he learnt that the famous bullfighter El Cordoble was staying in the same hotel! John Quinn went missing for a few days. It was discovered he had spent the time in the bathroom suffering from Montezuma's revenge! The tours helped to cement a great camaraderie and team spirit and it was Eric's reward after a season when his loyalty had been repaid. In the next chapter I go into detail regarding competing in Europe.

The players took great pride in playing competitively abroad but Eric provided the opportunity for them to play against undoubtedly the greatest player in the world at the time. Pele's Santos team from Brazil was invited to play a friendly at Hillsborough. It was a fantastic occasion, never forgotten by all who witnessed it. Pele and his Santos team would appear again at Hillsborough several years later, but the occasion didn't match that first game. It was subject to an early kick-off to avoid the use of floodlights, since the country at that time was in the grip of a recession that resulted in a three day working week. Thus, the attendance suffered but, once again, the game's greatest player had trodden the Hillsborough turf. Tommy Craig will always be grateful for that day as he was the first to rush up to Pele at the final whistle and swap shirts.

SHEFFIELD WEDNESDAY IN RUSSIA

SHEFFIELD WEDNESDAY TOUR OF RUSSIA
PLANE JUST LANDED AT MOSCOW AIRPORT 1960

Wednesday entourage after landing in Moscow

Provided courtesy of Derek Wilkinson

40

Cover of banquet programme to celebrate Wednesday's 5th appearance in an FA Cup Final, May 14th, 1966
Provided, courtesy of Isabel Brown

Programme cover for Wednesday v Santos 1962

Programme cover for Wednesday v Santos 1972 (Pele's second appearance at Hillsborough)
Both provided, courtesy of Andrew Cooper

Rule book issued to players for end of season tour to Russia, 1960

Programme cover and teams for game in Lenin Stadium against Moscow Torpedo

Provided courtesy of Derek Wilkinson

Lenin Stadium

Wednesday team lining up before game against Georgia Tbilisi

Rule book, fixtures, itinerary and entourage for end of season tour to Nigeria

Team photo before a game in Nigeria

Keith Ellis and Alan Finney relaxing in Nigeria

All provided courtesy of Derek Wilkinson.

CHAPTER SEVEN

THE EUROPEAN ADVENTURE

In 1955 the Inter City Fairs Cup competition was born after agreement between Stanley Rous of the English FA, a Swiss pools supremo and an Italian football administrator. All three would later become senior officials at FIFA. In its infancy the competition was meant to promote international trade fairs and was competed for by cities that held them regularly. The competition did not come under the auspices of UEFA until 1971 so until then the organisers virtually made the rules of entry into the competition on a season by season basis. Wednesday made their debut in the competition in the season of 1961/62, but several years previously Eric had made contact with one of the most influential figures in European football when he met Gigi Peronace in 1957. This meeting led to a personal friendship that lasted until Eric's death and was continued between the two families for years afterwards.

It is true to state that Gigi Peronace was the first football agent. In 1957 he had masterminded the transfer of John Charles from Leeds Utd to Juventus for £65,000. Charles received a signing-on fee of £10,000! Before this, he had negotiated transfers on behalf of Torino and Lazio and had acted as an interpreter for British managers in Italy.

After the signing of John Charles there was supposed to be a friendly between Leeds Utd and Juventus back at Elland Road. No doubt this was included in the transfer negotiations but for reasons unknown

Leeds Utd's board refused to sanction the game. Juventus were still keen to come to England so Gigi contacted Eric. Wednesday stepped into the breach and welcomed Juventus and John Charles to Hillsborough. The friendship was cemented. Gigi went on to negotiate the transfers of Jimmy Greaves, Joe Baker and Denis Law from British clubs to Italy and helped his old friend, Matt Busby, when Denis Law returned to England as a Manchester United player. So along with his circle of influential English friends in the game (Stanley Rous, Matt Busby, Bill Nicholson, Andrew Stephen to name but a few) Eric was now recognised as a visionary in the game on the European stage.

Wednesday went on to reach the quarter final in the Fairs Cup on their debut, falling to Barcelona, the beaten finalists. Hillsborough witnessed some great European nights in the 60s and fans had to wait a further 30 years before they could savour further European competition at this level when the club qualified for the Fairs Cup's successor, the UEFA Cup.

Programme cover and teams for friendly game, Wednesday v Juventus which saw John Charles appear in England for the first time since his transfer from Leeds United

Other programme covers and teams include games played by Wednesday against foreign opposition in the Inter City Fairs Cup: Barcelona, Roma

All provided courtesy of Derek Wilkinson.

FC Cologne and friendlies against foreign opposition: Moscow Torpedo (note the appearance of the great Lev Yashin), Werder Bremen and Napoli

All provided courtesy of Derek Wilkinson.

46

CHAPTER EIGHT

THE FOOTBALL MAN

Let's face it, a fan's priority is success on the field. Opinions will always differ but history tells us that Eric was responsible for breaking transfer records on four occasions. Eddie Quigley, Jackie Sewell, Albert Quixall and lastly Tommy Craig, who in 1969 became the costliest teenager on his move from Aberdeen. Eddie Quigley and Albert Quixall left the club and I think it's true to say, and certainly it's my opinion, that they were not missed. Jackie Sewell became an international after signing for Wednesday. Tommy Craig was a fabulous player who suffered the misfortune of having to play the majority of his career at Hillsborough when Wednesday were on a downward spiral. The team that finished runners up to Spurs for the League title in 1961 was Eric's team (bar Bobby Craig) in as much as they had all been signed by him.

Dennis Woodhead, a winger in the 1950s, was asked what Eric's team talks were like. His reply, as recounted by Roy Hattersley in his Foreword, was to the point and may sound belittling to today's coaching gurus but I think it sums up perfectly that generation of players. He said Eric would come into the dressing room at 2.50 pm and tell the lads 'Go out and do your best'! I can hear the young ones laughing now. As an ex-player myself, my head wasn't swimming with instructions and tactical formulae. It was a time before 4 - 2 - 4, 4 - 3 - 3. Players knew instinctively what they were supposed to do.

Don't misunderstand me, not for one minute am I suggesting that Eric would be a managerial success today but I am a true believer that natural talent is coached out of some modern players and this happens at an early age. Of course, the game today is much faster, equipment is lighter, pitches are drier and smoother but the game pre-1970s was more challenging in as much as conditions would vary greatly. Football today is more akin to a game of chess, i.e. which manager has the better tactical know-how. Fear of failure dominates their thinking. In the period I've covered here that fear did not exist. Of course, there was disappointment. Fans and players alike certainly didn't enjoy the experience of relegation in the yo-yo years but more often than not the next season was greeted with the same eternal optimism and that was appreciated by fans. I am talking about an era in the game when, excuse the pun, there was a level playing field.

It was not unknown for a team to be promoted to the top division and go on to win the title at the first attempt, as happened to Ipswich Town. Every club genuinely believed they were in with a chance of success. What a contrast today! If a club is promoted to the current top tier, mere survival at that level is judged a success!

CHAPTER NINE

THE VISIONARY

Eric was a demanding boss and he expected commitment and loyalty. He would be the first to say that there were other talented personnel and all of them were employed at Hillsborough for many years. Eric England succeeded Eric Taylor after his death. Isabel Brown was a loyal secretary and Ron Ward held his position as caretaker long after Eric passed away. There is no doubt that Eric created a family atmosphere.

The title of this chapter tells the reader what I think of Eric's ability. I truly believe that, as an administrator, he was ahead of his time. He realised at an early stage that modernising Hillsborough would lead to greater prestige not only for the club but for the city he loved. The ground has always been recognised as an important venue for big games but because Eric had travelled abroad he had seen stadia where supporters were obviously more comfortable, which in turn fostered a greater pride in their club.

When Harry Catterick took over team management Eric was determined to concentrate on ground improvements. He could rest easy after passing on a talented bunch of players to Catterick who stormed back to Division 1. The old wooden North Stand was demolished and in its place a 10,000 all seater, ultra modern, cantilever grandstand was erected. Every seat enjoyed an unobstructed view of the playing area. None other than Sir Stanley Rous officiated at the opening ceremony. Sir Stanley was a great friend of Eric and was only too pleased to attend. Hillsborough could now boast more seats than any other stadium outside Wembley! Semi-finals continued to be allocated and the increased seating was reflected in receipts to both the FA and Wednesday.

Eric however, was now thinking of bigger things. The FA was hoping England would be selected to host the 1966 World Cup and he was determined that Hillsborough would stage preliminary games in the competition. In preparation for this he travelled to Chile in 1962 to witness that country's staging of the competition. As a result of this meticulous research, not only was Hillsborough chosen to host the group stages in 1966, it also obtained funding from the FA for further ground improvements, which culminated in Leppings Lane being redeveloped. A new West Stand was erected which saw the disappearance of the much loved scoreboard, perched above the original, partially covered, standing area.

Everyone connected with the club was recovering from the adverse publicity following the bribes scandal. Wednesdayites could boast that Hillsborough was now a super stadium with a capacity of 65,000.

Eric's foresight and immaculate preparations, backed up by a brilliant backroom staff, were rewarded when Hillsborough was chosen as the best venue outside Wembley as the competition ended. On top of all this euphoria, the club had fought its way to Wembley themselves, to play Everton in the 1966 FA Cup Final curtain-raiser to the World Cup.

We all know about the disappointment of that game. Harry Catterick came up trumps against his old employer, but only after coming back from a two goal deficit, to triumph 3-2 in one of the most exciting Cup Finals ever seen at the famous stadium.

1966 would also witness another defining moment in Eric's career. That year the game was attempting to gain a foothold in North America. His reputation was such that he was offered the top administrative position in the fledgling North American Soccer League. The salary far exceeded anything he could earn in his home country but he rejected the offer.

As well as dedicating his time and effort to Sheffield Wednesday, Eric had other responsibilities. He was chairman of the Football League Secretaries and Managers Association. You will note the tributes paid to Eric on behalf of its members which appear in the Testimonial Match Magazine. He improved the members' pension scheme and provided advice and assistance to its younger members. In today's game, when it is all too common for a manager to lose his job, he should maybe spare a thought for Eric when he walks away with his compensation.

For most of Eric's career, player power was just a dream but he did witness the abolition of the maximum wage. However, he, along with other secretaries and managers in the top division, ensured that wages did not spiral out of control. In the guise of an unofficial cartel, the league placed another maximum of £30 per week. Again, I can hear our younger fans laughing, but £30 per week outstripped the average national wage. Eric also introduced a revolutionary bonus system for the players, which boosted their earnings and was based on points gained and attendances at home games. However, the cosy cartel was torn apart when the chairman of Fulham, Tommy Trinder, agreed to make Johnny Haynes the first £100 per week footballer in a blaze of publicity. The floodgates were opened and the football superstar was born.

I don't need to remind Wednesday fans about the desperate financial position the club finds itself in well into the 21st century. It's just a shame that Wednesday does not have the guidance, influence and prudent approach that Eric demonstrated so effectively. I shudder to think what he would make of the present state of his beloved Wednesday.

New North Stand under construction.
Photos taken by Eric. Provided courtesy of Robert Taylor.

A packed 3 sided Hillsborough.

Photos taken by Eric. Provided courtesy of Robert Taylor.

Programme cover and teams. Wednesday v Bolton Wanderers 23rd. August 1961.
The official opening of the new North Stand by Sir Stanley Rous.
Provided courtesy of Derek Wilkinson.

CHAPTER TEN

TRIBUTES

It was only fitting that the club Eric had served loyally for 45 years should pay its respects after his death. On 21st October 1974 a testimonial game between Wednesday and an England X1 was played in his honour. Don Revie had recently been appointed England team manager and was due to take charge of the national side for the first time the following week. Fans who attended were treated to a wonderful game of football and had the rare opportunity to watch the stars of the game in the flesh. The result was academic and the Wednesday team was beaten 5-0. The statisticians amongst you will recall that the club was relegated to the 3rd tier of football for the first time in its history at the end of the season. The game was attended by a host of famous names who were determined to pay their respects. The list of contributors to the match programme read like a football Hall of Fame. Nearer to home, Derek Dooley, Albert Quixall, Dennis Woodhead, Jackie Sewell, Roy Shiner, Ron Springett, Tom McAnearney and Redfearn Froggatt were all quoted.

SIR STANLEY ROUS (Former FIFA President) wrote: 'Eric was one of my closest friends and supporters while I was Secretary of the FA, President of the Fairs Cup (now UEFA Cup) competition, and President of FIFA. He was a man of vision and a most capable administrator and organiser. He readily undertook to organise representative matches and semi-finals in the FA Cup for the Football

Association. He was proud of his club and always sought opportunities to show its splendid facilities to visitors. I am sure he never had an enemy, and, judging by the tributes paid to him, his friends are legion'.

SIR MATT BUSBY wrote: 'Eric was a great friend and a great organiser, as I knew from personal experience. He always had a sense of humour, and even when under stress had a happy disposition. He made a great contribution to football'.

EDDIE QUIGLEY wrote: 'The only team that mattered to Eric was Wednesday. When you were joining them he made you feel you were signing for the No.1 club. If you wanted to leave you felt that he thought you were a fool for wanting to move from such a great club'.

In an earlier chapter I mentioned Eric's involvement in the Football League Secretaries' and Managers' Association which was founded in 1919 - an organisation that has gone from strength to strength and flourishes today under the leadership of another Sheffield footballing legend, Howard Wilkinson. RON GREENWOOD, acting chairman of the Association at the time, wrote: 'Eric was the man who persuaded me to join the SMA. I had said you just have to look after your own backyard in this game, but he told me I was wrong. He not only looked after Wednesday's backyard, but he helped other people look after their backyards, too'.

TED BATES wrote: 'Eric will be sadly missed by his many friends and colleagues in football, a game in which his knowledge was always held in the highest esteem. As chairman of the Football League SMA he worked ceaselessly on behalf of its members to improve the Football League Pension Scheme, finally succeeding, particularly to the great benefit of its younger members. A great champion of managers and the belief that those of stature should have the platform in the game from which to speak for its welfare. He gave a lot of time to people in the game, and he will be sadly missed'.

JOE MERCER wrote: 'When I was with Sheffield United I got to know Eric very well. In football he has always been recognised as a leading administrator, and his fellow managers will always remember him for what he did for our Association'.

BILL ANDERSON wrote: 'Eric was a little man, but he walked tall because he was respected and liked by everybody. He had more friends in the game than any other official'.

The most poignant tribute, in my opinion, came from a former player I had the pleasure of knowing when I was playing for the club in the Northern Intermediate League as a junior. KEITH BANNISTER had played for the Owls between 1946 and 1952 and returned to the club to coach the juniors. His tribute reads: 'Dedication was the name of Eric's game. He inspired a great pride in the club, so much so that there's still blue-and-white blood in my veins! He was a great psychologist, and knew how to handle people. Would that we could turn back the clock!'. For all Wednesdayites who remember Eric, that tribute, especially the last sentence, says it all.

ERIC ENGLAND, who succeeded his friend, spoke about a wonderfully gifted man who possessed a sense of humour which enabled him to overcome problems when they arose. Their friendship extended beyond their working lives.

The Yorkshire Television commentator KEITH MACKLIN announced that the broadcasting company would pay its own tribute by awarding a trophy named after Eric, to be competed for between Hallamshire FA and Sheffield and District Schools FA.

Here are the teams that competed on that memorable night.

ENGLAND SQUAD	WEDNESDAY SQUAD
Peter Shilton	Peter Springett
Alan Stevenson	Peter Rodrigues
Frank Lampard	Alan Thompson
Steve Whitworth	Danny Cameron
Willie Maddren	Jimmy Mullen
Dave Watson	Hugh Dowd
Martin Dobson	John Holsgrove
Billy Bonds	Ken Knighton
Colin Bell	Eric Potts
Tony Currie	Colin Harvey
Trevor Brooking	Brian Joicey
Rodney Marsh	Tommy Craig
Denis Tueart	Fred McIver
Frank Worthington	Bernard Shaw
Keith Weller	David Sunley

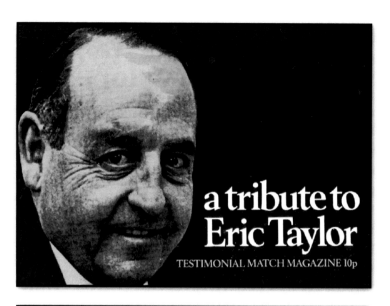

a tribute to
Eric Taylor
TESTIMONIAL MATCH MAGAZINE 10p

Mrs. Emmie Taylor wishes to thank all those people who have paid tribute to her late husband (and we have not been able to record them all), and to express her appreciation of the work and support given to the Testimonial by Sheffield Wednesday FC, the Football League Secretaries' and Managers' Association, and many others.

Cover of Eric's testimonial magazine and iconic image of Eric at his desk
All provided courtesy of Sheffield Wednesday

REVIE LOOKS FOR A TOP
CLASS TAYLOR TRIBUTE

By ANDREW TATHAM

A bu
baffli
sort o
week

e for Wednesday

Newspaper cuttings of game played between Wednesday and an England X1

Provided courtesy of Andrew Taylor

62

CHAPTER ELEVEN

REGRETS?

It's important to state that most of the regrets I list are my opinions based on what I have heard during my research; however, I know there is one that is definitely true.

It involves MY all time favourite player so I had to have a chuckle when the details came to light. Eric had signed Tommy Craig in 1969. Tommy became the costliest teenager in British football when he moved from Aberdeen (£100,000). A local journalist was keen to get the latest team news before a game (Tommy's debut against Tottenham in the last League game of season 1968/69) and asked Eric for this information. The reply came short and sharp, 'Tommy Craig and 10 others!'. There was no doubting Eric's sincerity but, on reflection, he should have known that this would upset other players, as well as increasing the pressure on young Tommy. One diplomatic faux pas in 40 years? Not bad! I finally caught up with Tommy who, along with his new team mates, was the innocent party in this incident and could be excused for feeling a little aggrieved. It was the first thing he recalled! However, he was determined to prove to Eric and the supporters that the record fee paid was money well spent. He went on to recall the great respect he had for Eric. He also went on to prove, yet again, that Eric could spot great talent. Tommy's time at Hillsborough coincided with Wednesday's fall from grace but he served the club loyally for 5 years before moving on and playing at a higher level.

Alan Finney played over 500 games for Wednesday. He received a £10 signing on fee after signing professional forms. He was a regular in three promotion seasons and helped Wednesday reach two FA Cup semi-finals. He was an ever present in the team that finished runners up to Spurs in 1960/61. It would be hard to recall a more loyal servant. Every player I have spoken to of his era said it was a travesty that Alan had not gained full international honours.

When Alan Brown made it abundantly clear that Alan Finney did not figure in his future plans he moved to his home town club, Doncaster Rovers. Don Megson, Gerry Young, Derek Wilkinson and Ron Springett were all granted testimonials; a well deserved thank you for long and loyal service.

Naturally, I asked Alan why he thought he had not received a testimonial. I had raised the issue when I met him. It says something about the man that he refused to complain but I could tell it hurt. Of all the players who merited a testimonial at Hillsborough I can't think of a more deserving case. Alan did point out that there was a testimonial held at Doncaster but the attendance and receipts were nowhere near those that would have been attained at Hillsborough. Alan was invited back to Hillsborough by the official supporters club who wished to pay their tributes to his magnificent service. Eric attended the function and Alan recalled him stating that he was one of the best players he had ever signed. Praise indeed!

Although Eric witnessed the halcyon years of the 1930s it must have been a major regret not to have seen Wednesday win more major honours. I believe that, in any other season than 1960/61, he would have witnessed the winning of the League championship with that team. It would have been truly deserved for the man who put that team together! Spurs were formidable and were the first team to complete the double that century. Perhaps a number of readers will say he should regret not allowing Catterick to sign Joe Baker but you won't be surprised to learn that I don't agree. I asked Derek Wilkinson what he thought of that old chestnut. His reply was music to my ears. 'Baker, no but if 'Bronco' Layne had been available at that time then Wednesday would have won the League title'.

CHAPTER TWELVE

HIS LEGACY

Without doubt Eric's greatest legacy is the stadium all Wednesdayites hold dear to their hearts. I have witnessed many changes at Hillsborough: two new grandstands, the covering of the Kop, renovation of the main stand and a conversion to an all seater stadium. After all these improvements, I firmly believe that Hillsborough still retains its character and lives up to the glowing accolade given by Simon Inglis in his book describing football league grounds (The Football Grounds of England and Wales, Collins/Willow, 1983).

The majority of modern stadia have no individual architectural feature and present a sterile appearance, normally surrounded by car parks and retail outlets. So the Hillsborough of today is Eric's tangible legacy. Even after the tragic events of 1989, Hillsborough went on to host internationals in the UEFA Euro competition in 1996. England's failure to be nominated to stage the 2018 World Cup has been a disappointment as the famous old ground would probably have hosted group games again.

Another legacy is one which will eventually disappear but until then will provide the talking points on which supporters thrive. That is the banter and endless discussions and arguments about players and events of the past. Opinions will always differ and these range from players' abilities to decisions taken by managers, chairmen and boards of directors.

My father is 89 years old and still waxes lyrical about Jackie Robinson and Jackie Sewell. I remember with great affection Albert Quixall, Alan Finney, Johnny Fantham, Ron Springett and Tommy Craig. All these players were signed by Eric. There were many more that I could mention and I apologise if a reader's favourite player has been omitted.

These players and their achievements in the game are testimony to the ability of Eric to spot a player and assess his potential. I hope I have proved that he was more than just a renowned administrator.

Perhaps one day Eric's great loyalty and service to Sheffield Wednesday will be honoured by having a part of Hillsborough named after him. As I said in my Introduction, it is unforgivable that this has not already happened.